A Guide to High-Tech Telescopes

Stargazing in Style

Table of Contents

Chapter 1. Introduction

Special Report Introduction:

Dip your toes into the awe-inspiring universe of high-tech telescopes with our exclusive special report, "A Guide to High-Tech Telescopes: Stargazing in Style." Don't let the technicality daunt you; we've made sure this guide is as reader-friendly as possible. Journey with us as we navigate the fascinating maze of cutting-edge technology, showcasing telescopes that empower even the amateur astronomer to explore celestial marvels. Whether you're an experienced stargazer or a novice yearning to delve into the cosmos, this comprehensive guide demystifies complex tech jargon, making it simple, relatable, and incredibly easy to equip yourself with the best stargazing instruments. Imagine, the thrill of diving deep into the glittering night sky could just be a few pages away! So buckle up and prepare for a joyride across the universe, all from the comfort of your backyard. This guide, dear reader, is your ticket to unlocking the mysteries of the firmament. Purchase this special report today and embark on an unforgettable cosmic adventure.

Chapter 2. A Telescope Primer: Understanding the Basics

Understanding the fundamental nature of telescopes and how they function is pivotal before diving into the intricacies of high-tech telescopes. By doing this, we establish a concrete base that would pave way for a comprehensive understanding down the line.

Telescopes, at their most fundamental level, are instruments that gather light. But how does this simple action lead us to comprehend the universe in its vast cosmological design? Let's begin to explore this marvel of human discovery and scientific trailblazing.

2.1. The Anatomy of a Telescope

A telescope, regardless of its technological advancements, comprises some essential components. Understanding these allows a basic comprehension of how telescopes operate:

1. **Objective:** This is responsible for gathering light. The objective could either be a lens (in the case of a refracting telescope) or a mirror (in a reflecting telescope). Suffice to say, the larger the objective, the better the scope's ability to collect light and deliver intricate details.

2. **Focal Length:** This pertains to the distance between the objective and the point where it focuses light (the focal point). The combination of an objective's diameter and focal length impact the telescope's ability to magnify an image.

3. **Eyepiece:** The eyepiece magnifies the image created by the objective at the focal point. It's important to remember that different eyepieces provide different levels of magnification and,

as such, are interchangeable for different viewing purposes.

4. **Mount:** Every telescope needs a solid base, termed a mount. These can swivel and angle to allow the viewing of different parts of the sky and to track celestial objects as the Earth rotates.

2.2. The Two Main Types of Telescopes

Telescopes can be broadly divided into two categories: refracting and reflecting. A refracting telescope uses objective lenses, whereas a reflecting telescope uses mirrors.

1. **Refracting Telescopes:** These telescopes employ lenses as their objectives. The lens bends or refracts light as it passes through, thus aligning it to a focal point where an image is formed. They tend to be long and slender, with an eyepiece at the opposite end of the objective lens. Refracting telescopes offer clear, sharp images making them suitable for viewing fine detail.

2. **Reflecting Telescopes:** These telescopes use mirrors to reflect light to a focal point. They offer large apertures and subsequently gather significantly more light than their refracting counterparts. This makes them ideal for the study of larger, dimmer celestial objects like galaxies and nebulae.

2.3. The Power of Magnification

One might assume that the more you magnify an image, the clearer it would be. This is a common misconception. Overdoing magnification can blur the image. A telescope's true power lies in its light-gathering capacity. The larger the diameter of the telescope's objective, the more light it can collect, enabling visibility of fainter objects, and extracting more detail from brighter celestial bodies.

2.4. The Magic of Refraction and Reflection

We see objects because they either emit or reflect light into our eyes. Telescopes collect significantly larger amounts of this light, focusing it into a point where a magnified image of the object can be seen. The methods of collection vary:

1. **Refraction:** When light passes from one medium into another (from air to glass in this case), it changes direction; a process known as refraction. This principle is utilised to bring light from a broad area to focus within a small area.

2. **Reflection:** A mirror reflects light that falls onto it. Curved mirrors, like those in a reflecting telescope, send this reflected light to a focused point. Due to their easier and cheaper production methods, large mirror lenses are commonly found in powerful professional telescopes.

2.5. Choosing the Right Telescope

When trying to select the best telescope, one needs to consider many factors such as your observing interests, location, and budget. Physical factors like stability, portability, assembly, and ease of use should also be contemplated.

For observing details on the moon, bright planets, or double stars, a refracting telescope or a compound telescope (which combines refraction and reflection) would be suitable. However, for more deep sky observing like galaxies and nebulae, larger reflecting telescopes are recommended due to their light-gathering power.

Remember, the best telescope is the one you use most often! The universe is full of wonders, and with the right telescope, they are all within your reach.

As the famous astronomer Galileo Galilei once said, "All truths are easy to understand once they are discovered; the point is to discover them." By developing our understanding of the fundamental workings of telescopes, we are well on our way to discover our mysterious cosmos. In the upcoming chapters, we will delve into the high-tech universe of telescopes. So, arm yourself with patience, persistence, and a thirst for heavenly knowledge, and let this primer serve as your stepping stone to a cosmic journey like no other!

Chapter 3. The Evolution of Telescopes: From Galileo to Digital

From a rudimentary tool devised by the great mind of Galileo Galilei to the digital age marvels that captivate us today, telescopes have undergone significant transformation. Their evolution has been inextricably intertwined with humanity's insatiable urge to decipher the vast expanse of the cosmos, an endeavor that culminated in the creation of devices capable of peering into distant galaxies and nebulae.

3.1. The Birth of the Telescope: Galileo's Implement

Galileo Galilei's telescope, invented circa 1608, was a simple, refracting device that utilized a convex objective lens and a concave eyepiece, a design fundamentally different from the 'spyglasses' of that era. Though it had a mere 20x magnification, this tool introduced us to a universe brimming with celestial wonders, breaking free from the traditional worldview.

Galileo's observations, including the moon's craters, Jupiter's moons, and Venus' phases, using his primitive but revolutionary telescope, altered our understanding of the cosmos and cemented the instrument's place in astronomy.

3.2. Early Advances: Newton's Reflector

In 1672, Isaac Newton enhanced the design by inventing the

reflecting telescope, mitigating the inherent issue of chromatic aberration that plagued refracting models. Integrating a concave primary mirror to bundle incoming light, and a flat secondary mirror to direct the light to the eyepiece, this advancement improved clarity and ensured a more accurate representation of celestial objects. This design, albeit refined and miniaturized, continues in modern devices today.

3.3. Dormant Period and the Rise of Speculum Mirrors

Telescope technology experienced a dormant period after Newton until William Herschel's era in the late 18th century. His contribution was notable; elevating the Newtonian telescope design by introducing larger speculum (metal) mirrors which increased magnification capabilities exponentially.

However, the laborious process of polishing speculum mirrors coupled with their low reflectivity (merely 2/3rds of the incident light was reflected) and tendency to tarnish quickly made them less desirable. This led to the advent of glass mirrors coated with tin or silver, enhancing reflectivity to nearly 90%.

3.4. Astrophotography and Spectroscopy: Expeditions into the Unknown

The 19th century experienced significant telescope modification with photographic capabilities and spectroscopy integrated into telescope designs. Astrophotography, the practice of photographing celestial bodies, began in 1840 with the daguerreotype camera.

Spectroscopy, the scientific procedure of using a prism to split light into its constituent colors, enabled astronomers to analyze the chemical composition of stars, furthering our understanding of the cosmic fabric. In 1868, Norman Lockyer used spectroscopy to discern the chemical signature of a previously unknown element in the sun, which he named Helium.

3.5. The Radio Revolution: The Invisible Spectrum

1937 marked a radical departure in telescope technology with Grote Reber's radio telescope. Unlike conventional telescopes that observed visible light, Reber's innovation captured radio waves emitted by celestial bodies. The radio telescope delved into a new realm, introducing the study of quasars, pulsars, cosmic microwave background radiation, and more.

3.6. Hubble Space Telescope: Observing from the Heavens

Launched in 1990, the Hubble Space Telescope revolutionized astronomy by orbiting outside Earth's murky atmosphere. It could capture incredibly sharp images across a broad light spectrum. Free from atmospheric distortions, it opened a window to the universe that no ground-based telescope could achieve, deepening our understanding of galaxies, nebulae, and other celestial phenomena.

3.7. From Analogue to Digital: The Evolution Continues

The advent of digital technology added another layer to the telescope's evolution. CCD (Charge-Coupled Device) cameras, with their superior sensitivity to light and capability to digitize images, greatly enhanced the power of telescopes. Astronomers could now observe faint galaxies billions of light-years away, an unthinkable achievement in Galileo's time.

Moreover, modern telescopes adopted go-to systems, mechanisms pre-loaded with coordinates of thousands of celestial objects. This allowed even the beginners to navigate the night sky effortlessly, democratizing the stargazing experience.

3.8. The Future: From James Webb to the Event Horizon Telescope

As we stand on the brink of the James Webb Space Telescope's deployment, whose infrared sensitivity will let us peer through cosmic dust clouds into stellar nurseries, we realize the journey is far from over.

Simultaneously, advancements like the Event Horizon Telescope employ a global network of radio antennas to function as an Earth-sized interferometer, garnering a first-ever image of a black hole. These remarkable feats underscore the ceaseless evolution of telescopes, revealing the universe's unfathomable depths and beauty.

The quest to chronicle the universe, from its legendary constellations to its mysterious dark matter, spurs the evolution of the telescope. The story of telescopes is etched in our pursuit of cosmic knowledge—a testament to humanity's innate curiosity and resilience.

Chapter 4. Decoding Technical Terms: A Layman's Guide

In the world of astronomy and telescopes, technical terms can often seem like a foreign language. Here, we aim to give you the comfort of fluency.

4.1. The Basics: Key Telescope Components

Before diving into the high-tech aspects of telescopes, it's important to understand the basic parts of these devices.

- **Aperture:** Aperture, simply put, is the diameter of the main lens or mirror in a telescope. Measured in millimeters (mm) or inches, it determines how much light the telescope can collect. A larger aperture allows a telescope to capture more light, leading to clearer images.

- **Focal Length:** The distance from the telescope's main lens or mirror to the spot where the light rays come together is called focal length. Generally, a telescope with a longer focal length provides higher magnification but a narrower field of view.

- **Eyepiece:** The eyepiece works like a magnifying glass, enlarging the image produced by the aperture and focal length. These are important components that influence the telescope's magnifying power.

- **Mount:** The telescope's mount acts like a tripod, supporting the device and allowing it to move in various directions. There are two main types – altazimuth (moves up, down, left, and right) and equatorial (tracking the rotation of the night sky).

- **Finder Scope:** This is a small, low-power telescope mounted on the main telescope. It has a wide field of view to aid in locating objects and centering them in the main telescope's field of view.

4.2. High-Tech Telescope Terminology

Having covered the basics, let's delve into the high-tech specifics.

- **GOTO Systems:** Modern telescopes often come equipped with computerized GOTO systems. This feature enables the telescope to automatically move to, and track, specific celestial objects after the user inputs their coordinates or selects them from a built-in database.

- **Apochromatic (APO) and Achromatic Refractors:** These denote types of refractors, which are telescopes that use lenses. Achromatic refractors use two lenses to reduce, but not eliminate, color fringing. APO refractors, being more advanced, mostly eliminate color fringing by using three lenses.

- **Dobsonian Telescopes:** Named after the amateur astronomer John Dobson, these are a type of altazimuth-mounted Newtonian reflector telescope. They are known for their ease of use, low cost, and capability to view faint deep sky objects due to larger apertures.

4.3. Understanding Telescope Formats

Telescopes come in many formats, and understanding these is crucial.

- **Refractor Telescopes:** These use lenses to gather and focus light. They provide high-contrast images and require minimal maintenance.

- **Reflector Telescopes:** Also known as Newtonian Reflectors, these use mirrors instead of lenses. They are more affordable and provide wider fields of view but require frequent alignment (also known as collimating) of their mirrors.

- **Catadioptric or Compound Telescopes:** These use a combination of lenses and mirrors to fold optics and create an image. Two popular types are the Schmidt-Cassegrain and the Maksutov-Cassegrain.

4.4. The Magnification Myth

One common misconception is that magnification (often touted in advertisements) is the most important characteristic of a telescope. This, however, is not true. Instead, the aperture size and overall optical quality of the telescope matter the most. Poor optics with high magnification lead to blurry images. Remember that a clear, bright image without magnification is more desirable than a large, blurred one.

4.5. Deciphering Specifications

Every telescope comes with certain specifications mentioned. Here's your guide to understanding these.

- **Focal Ratio (f/number):** The focal ratio is the focal length divided by the aperture. It gives an idea of image brightness and field of view.

- **Magnification (Power):** The magnification of a telescope can be calculated by dividing the focal length of the telescope by the focal length of the eyepiece. Standard eyepieces usually offer magnifications between 40x and 200x.

- **Field of View:** The amount of sky visible at once through the telescope is termed as the field of view.

- **Resolving Power:** This is the ability of a telescope to distinguish between two close points of light.

- **Limiting Magnitude:** The faintest star a telescope can see under perfect conditions is its limiting magnitude.

4.6. The Computerized Telescope Revolution

Computerization has revolutionized telescopes. With features such as automatic tracking and finding, databases of celestial objects, GPS, WiFi, and remote control functions, stargazing has become significantly easier, especially for beginners.

Although these high-tech telescopes can take some time to get used to, they offer extensive capabilities, making astronomy more accessible to everyone.

Whether you're looking to invest in your first telescope or upgrade to a more advanced model, remember to consider the terminology and specifications discussed here. With this newfound understanding, the complex world of telescopes can become a friendly companion in your journey through the stars.

Chapter 5. Types of High-Tech Telescopes: How to Choose What's Right for You

Telescopes have advanced significantly since their inception and today's devices bring the cosmos within everyone's reach. Choosing the best high-tech telescope can be daunting, especially with the various types available. In this detailed guide, we will discuss the different types of high-tech telescopes and offer tips on how to decide which is the best fit for you.

5.1. Refracting Telescopes

One of the earliest telescope designs, the refracting or refractor, uses two lenses to gather and focus light. Its design is straightforward and typically very reliably built. The main lens, or objective lens, sits at the front and light gets refracted or bent as it passes through this lens. This bending of light toward the center forms an image at the point of focus.

Refracting telescopes are famed for their sharp image quality and are perfect for viewing the moon, planets, and double stars. They require little to no maintenance, which makes them excellent for beginners. However, be aware of chromatic aberration - the failure of the lens to bring all wavelengths of color to the same focal plane, which can result in a blurry image.

Common types of refractor telescopes include **Achromatic Refractors** and **Apochromatic Refractors** (or "Apos"). An Achromatic refractor uses two lenses to significantly reduce chromatic aberration, while an Apochromatic refractor uses multiple lenses to eliminate it altogether, hence providing the finest image quality among refractor telescopes.

5.2. Reflecting Telescopes

Reflecting or reflector telescopes take a different approach from refractors. A large mirror replaces the objective lens used in refractors, which collects light and focuses it onto a secondary mirror that further redirects the light to the eyepiece.

Reflecting telescopes offer various advantages: they are cost-effective (since it's cheaper to produce a large mirror than a large lens) and virtually eliminate chromatic aberration. Because of their typically larger aperture, they are excellent deep-sky viewing platforms for nebulae, galaxies, and star clusters.

Notable types include **Newtonian Reflectors** - named after their creator, Sir Isaac Newton - and **Dobsonian Reflectors**.

A Newtonian reflector telescope's primary mirror is parabolic, which means it is capable of collecting light and focusing it to a single point. Dobsonian telescopes, on the other hand, are a type of altazimuth-mounted Newtonian reflector. They are simple, high-capacity deep-sky 'light buckets'.

Keep in mind that reflecting telescopes require occasional maintenance, including realigning the mirrors (collimation) and removing dust.

5.3. Compound or Catadioptric Telescopes

Compound or Catadioptric telescopes, such as the Schmidt-Cassegrain, incorporate both lenses and mirrors, taking advantage of the best aspects of refracting and reflecting telescopes. They offer compact portable designs, versatility in usage, and relatively lower maintenance than reflectors.

Compound telescopes can be used for both astronomical and terrestrial viewing, and are excellent for observing finer details on the Moon and planets. They're also good for deep-sky observation. However, they are typically more expensive than their refractor and reflector counterparts.

Models include **Maksutov-Cassegrains** and **Schmidt-Cassegrains**. Maksutov-Cassegrains are esteemed for their sharp, high-contrast view, while Schmidt-Cassegrains are revered for their versatility and portability.

5.4. Radio Telescopes and Space Telescopes

While not generally for personal use, these telescopes are the zenith of observing technology. **Radio Telescopes** observe radio waves from space, broadening our view beyond just visible light. These arrays can span across continents, exemplified by the Very Long Baseline Array (VLBA).

Space Telescopes like the Hubble and the upcoming James Webb telescope, free from atmospheric disturbances, provide the clearest, most detailed observations of the universe.

Now when choosing which telescope is right for you, consider factors such as cost, maintenance, portability, and specifically what you aim to observe. Each telescope type excels in different areas. For instance, refractors are perfect for planets, while large reflectors are deep-sky observation savants.

While the sheer choice can feel overwhelming, remember that there's no wrong decision. Go forth, channel your inner Galileo, and delve into the mysteries of the universe. You are, after all, made of stardust!

Chapter 6. Top-of-the-line Telescopes: Exploring the Market Leaders

Our voyage into the mesmerizing world of high-tech telescopes begins with an exploration of industry leaders. Several renowned telescope manufacturers have earned their reputation for bringing cutting-edge technology to the masses. Understanding the offerings of these companies is key to finding the ideal tool for your stargazing needs.

6.1. The Goliath of the Astronomy World: Celestron

One name that stands out in the industry is Celestron. Known for creating sleek, powerful telescopes, Celestron brings a range of options to all levels of stargazing enthusiasts, from beginners to advanced users.

For beginners passionate about unraveling the mysteries of the universe, Celestron offers the Astro Fi 5, a WiFi-enabled Schmidt-Cassegrain telescope that leverages Stellarium software to locate celestial bodies. This scope, with its GoTo mount that automatically points the telescope to desired stars, planets, or galaxies, proves an absolute charm for rookie astronomers. The telescope also contends with light pollution reasonably well for its size, ensuring a clearer view of the night sky.

For mid-level enthusiasts, the NexStar 8 SE is a worthwhile mention. This scope has a computerized altazimuth mount and a database of more than 40,000 celestial bodies. It also boasts SkyAlign technology, which simplifies the alignment and allows the stellar enthusiast to explore celestial objects with precision.

For the advanced users, Celestron Evolution series takes the pie. The Evolution 9.25 EdgeHD is a sophisticated compound telescope with built-in wifi, StarBright XLT optical coatings for maximum light gathering, and an inbuilt lithium-ion battery that can juice up your stargazing sessions for up to 10 hours.

"Remember: the telescope's aperture size plays a vital role in determining the clarity and detail of the image. Bigger aperture means higher resolution, allowing you to see increasingly faint objects." [/note]

6.2. Meade Instruments: Innovative Designs, Practical Pricing

Another market leader, Meade, has also captured the heart of the stargazing community. They're known for marrying innovation with practical pricing, making high-quality astronomy gear accessible to a more extensive range of users.

The Meade ETX80 Observer – a compact, portable refractor telescope – is a beginner's delight. It comes with an AudioStar handbox controller equipped with a database of over 30,000 celestial objects, letting you pinpoint them with ease. Its achromatic lens minimizes chromatic aberration and guarantees you clear, bright images.

In the mid-range category, the LX90-ACF stands out. This advanced Coma-Free (ACF) Catadioptric telescope sports an impressive altazimuth mount, built-in GPS, and 30,000 object-database for seamless stargazing experiences. It's accurate, user-friendly, and enjoyable to use.

For the seasoned observer, the LX600-ACF is a must-consider. Its fast f/8 Advanced Coma-Free optics, StarLock full-time automatic guiding, and ultrahigh transmission coatings promise not only clear, crisp images but also precise tracking and speedy setup.

6.3. Sky-Watcher: Master of Dobsonian Telescopes

Sky-Watcher enjoys a high reputation for manufacturing the finest Dobsonian telescopes. Their products fall into various categories, ranging from beginner-friendly to advanced, specialized equipment.

The Heritage 150P Flextube is pitched to beginners and intermediates. Its stable and straightforward operation, combined with its large 150mm aperture, enables users to have a satisfying glimpse of faint galaxies, nebulae, and star clusters.

The Sky-Watcher Flextube 300P SynScan Dobsonian stands as the hallmark of their advanced category. With a massive 12-inch aperture and automated GoTo capabilities with SynScan hand controller and database of 42,900 night sky objects, it permits a detailed exploration of deep-sky objects.

6.4. Wrap Up

Choosing the right telescope requires taking into account factors such as budget, portability, set-up, maintenance, and advanced features. Remember, the perfect telescope for you is one that aligns with your level of experience, needs, and aspirations. As you read through this guide, remember to stay connected with your purpose: the thrill of exploring the night sky. No matter where your journey takes you, purchase a telescope that resonates with your love of celestial exploration and let it guide you through the vast universe.

Chapter 7. Telescope Features: A Closer Look at Capabilities and Functionality

In the grand quest to unravel the cosmos and bask in its exquisite marvels, high-tech telescopes are the stargazer's trusted companions. And like any good sidekick, the strength of these valuable tools lies in their wealth of features, intricacies, and capabilities. Let's take a journey to understand these components better and see how they add functionality to your space exploration endeavor.

7.1. Aperture: The Gatekeeper of Light

Aperture refers to the diameter of a telescope's light-gathering lens or mirror, often known as the objective. Measured in millimeters or inches, a larger aperture allows a telescope to absorb more light, thereby rendering sharper and brighter images. It may surprise novice stargazers to learn that a telescope's power lies not in its magnification, but in its aperture size. A larger aperture ensures superior resolution, permitting the observer to discern finer details and see fainter objects.

7.2. Focal Length: Enhancing Magnification

The focal length of a telescope is the distance (typically measured in millimeters) from the objective lens or mirror to the point where the telescope is focused. It directly influences the magnification and field of view. Generally speaking, telescopes with a longer focal length provide larger magnification. However, they also offer a narrower field of view. This principle is best explained by comparing a telescope to a zoom lens on a camera: the higher the 'zoom,' the narrower the field of view. Shrewd stargazers manipulate their telescope's focal length to best match their observational objectives.

7.3. Mounts: The Unsung Hero

Mounts are the unsung heroes of the telescopic world and are crucial for a steady and smooth stargazing experience. Altazimuth and Equatorial are the two primary types.-

- Altazimuth Mounts operate on a simple two-axis system - horizontal (azimuth) and vertical (altitude). They're straightforward to use and great for terrestrial observing as well as casual stargazing.

- Equatorial Mounts, while initially complex, are precisely aligned with Earth's axis of rotation. Using just one axis (right ascension), they follow the apparent path of the stars as Earth rotates, providing much-needed stability for extended or astrophotographic observations.

7.4. Finderscopes: Navigating the Starry Sea

Much like a ship's first mate guiding it safely through treacherous seas, a finderscope is a small, low-power telescope mounted alongside the primary telescope. It showcases a larger field of view, helping stargazers accurately locate and center objects. The two styles are reflex sight and optical finderscope:

- Reflex Sights project a tiny illuminated targeting dot or circle onto a clear, wide-view window.

- Optical Finderscopes function similarly to the main telescope but exhibit a less magnified field of view.

7.5. Eyepieces: The Personal Detailer

Eyepieces, small and easy to overlook, are vital parts of your telescopic arsenal. They're your personal detailers, working closely with your telescope's focal length to magnify the image formed at the focal point. An array of eyepieces is readily available, allowing for different magnifications. Remember, the higher the magnification, the lesser the field of view. It's always wise to strike a balance based on what you aim to observe.

7.6. Telescope Types: Reflectors, Refractors, and Compound Telescopes

Finally, deciding upon the type of telescope itself is an essential ascent in your stargazing journey. There are three primary kinds you'll encounter: Reflectors, Refractors, and Compound Telescopes:

- Reflector Telescopes, invented by Isaac Newton, use mirrors to gather and focus light. They're great for viewing celestial bodies like galaxies and nebulae and famous for their affordability.

- Refractor Telescopes, with their superior lenses, offer sharper images and are ideal for viewing planets and the moon. They're easy to maintain but can be more expensive, especially with larger apertures.

- Compound or Catadioptric Telescopes integrate both lenses and mirrors to fold optics and form an image. Compact and versatile, these telescopes are perfect for viewing bright and far-off celestial bodies.

To conclude, the stargazing journey requires a firm understanding of telescope jargon. To glide smoothly through the fascinating field of celestial navigation, recognizing the importance of each telescope component is crucial. Together, they shape your experience, ensuring that each star, nebula, or galaxy can be precisely pinpointed and marveled at, right from your backyard. As you delve deeper into this guide, you'll begin to comprehend how to choose and finetune these features to witness the cosmos in its complete glory.

Chapter 8. Stargazing in Style: Innovations in Telescope Design and Accessorizing

In the realm of stargazing, the telescope plays the part of a magic wand, unlocking secrets of the cosmos that are hidden from the naked eye. Over the past decades, significant technological strides have made these mystical tools more sophisticated, more accurate, and more accessible, even to novices gazing starward for the first time. As telescope technology rapidly evolves, so too does the diversity of designs and accessories, each providing unique means to delve deeper into the mysteries of the universe.

8.1. Treading the Path of Innovation: Evolving Telescope Designs

The evolution of telescope designs has aimed at enhancing performance, refining the user interface, and increasing portability. The following section offers an in-depth overview of some pioneering designs that have reinvented the stargazing experience.

Dobsonian Telescopes \n John Dobson revolutionized the world of amateur astronomy when he birthed the design of a simple yet powerful alt-azimuth mount telescope, now eponymously dubbed the Dobsonian telescope. Favoring ease of use and facility of construction over other features, Dobsonian telescopes illuminate the night sky with a large objective lens, capturing bright images of distant celestial bodies, all at an affordable price.

However, it also comes with its quirks. Its alt-azimuth mount allows movement along the vertical and horizontal axes but lacks automatic tracking. But, with accessories like an equatorial platform, you can afford the Dobsonian the benefit of automatic tracking.

Schmidt-Cassegrain Telescopes \n Offering a balanced amalgamation of image quality, compactness, and versatility, the Schmidt-Cassegrain Telescope (SCT) embraces a compound design. It leverages mirrors and lenses to fold the path of light, effectively packing a long focal length into a short tube. SCTs are a wise bet for observers invested in both terrestrial and celestial viewing, astrophotography, or who seek a portable all-rounder.

Ritchey-Chrétien Telescopes \n Highly favored in the realm of astrophotography, the Ritchey-Chrétien Telescope (RCT) has a dual hyperbolic mirror design. This unique configuration minimizes distortions like coma and field curvature, thereby providing pinpoint star images across the entire field of view. However, these benefits come at a steeper price and more complex alignment procedures, making RCTs better suited to experienced stargazers and astrophotographers.

The choice of a telescope design would ultimately depend on your celestial aspirations.

8.2. Looking Through a Lens: Ancillary Marvels of Telescope Accessories

Telescope enhancements have concurrently evolved, making way for an expansive range of accessories, each moving toward refining your stargazing journey.

Eyepieces \n The eyepiece acts as the command center of your viewing experience. There's a wide variety of eyepiece designs -

Plossl, Orthoscopic, and the cutting-edge Ethos by Tele Vue, with each offering different levels of magnification, clarity, and field of view. When choosing an eyepiece, consider the specifications of your telescope, and the celestial bodies you wish to observe.

Filters \n Much like their photographic counterparts, telescope filters play a crucial role in improving image visibility and contrast. With a proper filter attached, stargazers can observe the finer details of celestial structures, such as the surface of the moon or the cloud bands of Jupiter. Some filters can also help to diminish the effects of light pollution, improving the urban sky-watcher's experience.

Mounts \n Telescope mounts, though often overlooked, are key to comfortable and effective stargazing. While alt-azimuth mounts offer easy, intuitive motion, equatorial mounts, with their motor-driven tracking, are preferred for astrophotography and observing fast-moving objects. GOTO mounts, interlaced with databases of celestial bodies, improve object locating and tracking, thus increasing the convenience for novice astronomers.

Telescope Cameras \n For those looking to capture their stargazing experiences, a good astrophotography camera is crucial. Depending on your expertise and needs, there are options ranging from simple planetary cameras to advanced, cooled, monochrome CCD cameras. Remember to account for your telescope's specifications and your own astrophotography goals when choosing a camera.

This chapter offered an exhaustive exploration of the myriad design evolutions and accessorizing options in the realm of high-tech telescopes. Between the lines, we hope these details illuminate your journey, as you navigate the thrilling vistas of stargazing, armed with knowledge and bolstered by technological marvels. Blending science, technology, and passion, modern stargazing offers a more accessible, personal, and profound engagement with our celestial neighbours, making each step and each swirling star feel a little closer to home.

Chapter 9. Introduction to Astro-Imaging: Capture the Cosmos

In the world of astronomy, capturing the celestial spectacle using modern telescope technology is no less than an art form. This intricate process, known as astro-imaging, turns hours spent under the chilly night sky into dazzling visuals of cosmic wonders. Here, we will explore in depth the techniques, the technological underpinnings of this art, the challenges, and the rewarding outcomes it presents.

With the onset of digital photography and advanced astronomical equipment, astro-imaging has made significant leaps, enabling amateurs and experienced stargazers alike to behold and capture the cosmos like never before.

9.1. What is Astro-Imaging?

Astro-imaging is the practice of capturing images of celestial objects. It often involves a variety of advanced equipment including telescopes, mounts, cameras, and software. Astro-imaging can range from simple shots of moon phases to deep-sky imaging of galaxies, nebulae, and star clusters. In recent years, thanks to advancements in digital technology, the barrier to entry has significantly decreased, making it an accessible hobby for the majority.

9.2. Astro-Imaging versus Astrophotography

The terms astro-imaging and astrophotography are often used interchangeably. While they are closely related, there are subtle differences. A key divergence is the medium; astrophotography traditionally refers to capturing images on film, while astro-imaging refers to digital capture. Moreover, astro-imaging typically implies a more extensive post-processing technique, creating an image that often goes beyond the capabilities of a single frame of film.

9.3. The Right Equipment for Astro-Imaging

Embarking on the journey of astro-imaging requires access to a suite of specialized equipment designed to work harmoniously to capture the cosmos's true beauty. 1. Telescope: The choice of telescope matters. A refractor telescope is recommended due to its higher contrast, eliminating issues around diffraction spikes that catadioptric telescopes might have. 2. Mount: A motorized mount that can track the movement of celestial bodies is required for clear, prolonged exposures. 3. Camera: A dedicated astro-imaging camera is preferred over a DSLR, as it's cooled, reducing noise that often spoils long-exposure shots. 4. Filters: Light pollution filters can be a lifesaver in areas with high light pollution, assisting you in bringing out the best of your shots. 5. Software: Image processing software is essential for stacking and post-processing captured images.

9.4. Essential Techniques in Astro-Imaging

Astro-imaging is not just about the equipment but also the techniques employed. Here, we walk you through the key techniques that every astro-imager needs to master.

9.4.1. Polar Alignment

Polar alignment is a crucial step in the setup process for astro-imaging. It involves aligning your telescope's mount with the Earth's axis of rotation, a procedure that enables your setup to accurately track celestial objects across the sky. Without correct polar alignment, your images might suffer from field rotation, which can turn potentially stunning shots into unintelligible smudges of light.

9.4.2. Auto-guiding

Auto-guiding is a process which greatly enhances the tracking accuracy of your pictures. The auto-guiding system, attached to the mount or through a second telescope, follows a guide star's movement and continually corrects for any error in the mount's tracking. The result is sharper images with pin-point stars, a trait often desired by all astro-imagers.

9.4.3. Focus and Coma Correction

Achieving a sharp focus is crucial for good astro-images. Some digital cameras offer a Live View focusing aid, which provides a magnified view of a star to assist in focusing. Furthermore, correcting coma, an optical aberration causing elongated stars towards the edge of the image, is equally important. Combating this requires a coma corrector which is usually inserted into the telescope's optical path before the camera.

9.4.4. Stacking and Post Processing

Astro-imaging involves exposure to low-light circumstances, often leading to an abundance of image noise. This can be overcome by capturing multiple exposures of the same object and stacking them, a process that averages out the random noise, providing a high signal-to-noise ratio. Post-processing techniques include adjusting the contrast, brightness, and color levels to reveal hidden details within the image.

Astro-imaging is a thrilling intersection of science, technology, and art. Though the path to capturing striking celestial images is an involved process, the rewards are immense. Each clear, sparkling image of the cosmos is a personal souvenir of the universe, a testament to human curiosity and a tangible connection to the amazing universe in which we live. By understanding the intricacies of astro-imaging, you empower yourself to embark on this incredible journey of cosmic exploration. Who knows? The next image you capture might not only inspire you but also instill the love for astronomy in others.

Chapter 10. Maintenance Tips for Long-lasting Telescopes

Proper maintenance of your telescope ensures not only a long and fruitful life of your instrument but also the quality and clarity of your celestial observations. With mindful upkeep, your telescope can continue to open up the wonders of the universe for you for many years.

10.1. Understanding the Telescope Structure

Before embarking on maintenance, it is imperative to understand your telescope's structure. Telescopes generally consist of an optical tube, mount, and accessories such as eyepieces. While each component requires its attention, they all need general cleaning and correct storage to avoid damage.

The optical tube, where the optics (either lenses or mirrors) are housed, is the heart of a telescope. Keeping the optics free from dust and debris is paramount to maintaining the visual quality of the device. Bear in mind that what counts as proper maintenance for lenses may be different from that for mirrors.

The mount and tripod provide the stability your telescope needs to focus on distant objects in the sky. Whether it's an altazimuth mount (moving in altitude - up and down; azimuth - side-to-side) or an equatorial mount (aligned with the Earth's axis of rotation), each has its care requirements.

Finally, telescope accessories such as eyepieces, Barlow lenses, filters, or adapters enhance the functionality of your telescope. Each component has its care guidelines to ensure they play their roles effectively.

10.2. Cleaning the Telescope's Optics

Common sense might suggest that the more frequently you clean your optics, the better. However, too frequent or incorrect cleaning can harm these delicate surfaces. Therefore, the rule of thumb for telescope maintenance is: clean the optics as rarely as possible and only when necessary.

However, the inevitable buildup of dust requires eventual maintenance. Here are some step-by-step suggestions on how to clean the device's optics correctly:

1. Ensure dust is not wiped off the surface with a dry cloth as this could result in troublesome scratches. Instead, use an air blower or camel's hair brush to gently remove particulates.

2. For smudges or stubborn dirt, apply a small amount of specially formulated lens cleaning solution (never use household cleaning products) to a lint-free wipe or cotton ball and carefully clean the optics in a circular motion.

3. If your telescope uses mirrors (Newtonian/Dobsonian reflector), do not remove them from their cell for cleaning. Instead, use distilled water with a drop of dish soap. Rinse thoroughly and let air dry.

4. Before storing the telescope, assure the optics are entirely dry to avoid fungal growth.

10.3. Attending to the Mount and Tripod

Maintaining the telescope mount can be equally as crucial as taking care of the optics. Both altazimuth and equatorial mounts have their specifics, but the following guidelines apply to both:

1. As with the optics, dust can also cause damage to the mount. Use a blower to remove dust from the surface. For an equatorial mount, pay special attention to the counterweights and their shaft.

2. Lubricating the moving parts of the mount can ensure smooth motion. Use a high-quality silicone-based lubricant, remembering not to overdo it.

3. As for the tripod, confirm all nuts and bolts are tight but avoid over-tightening as that can wear down the threads over time.

10.4. Care of Telescope Accessories

Finally, don't neglect the care of your accessories. They amplify the function of your telescope, and their upkeep is equally important.

1. Always replace caps or cases on your eyepieces, Barlow lenses, and filters when they're not in use.

2. Clean these accessories using the guidelines provided for lens care. However, keep in mind that smaller lenses, such as eyepieces, can be tricky to clean, and it may be safer and relatively inexpensive to replace rather than clean them.

10.5. The Right Way to Store Your Telescope

Properly storing your telescope can significantly minimize upkeep requirements and increase its longevity. Adhering to these tips ensures safe storage when the equipment is not in use:

1. Store the telescope in a cool, dry place free from dust and humidity. A protective case or cover will be of great utility.

2. Even when stored, check on your telescope regularly to confirm no dust or fungus is affecting the optics or other components.

10.6. Upkeep Is Not Just About Cleaning

Apart from cleaning, tuning your telescope every so often can keep it in the finest operating condition. Regular minute adjustments to the alignment (collimation) of your device can considerably enhance your viewing experience.

To conclude, a telescope, like any sophisticated device, needs adequate maintenance. Remember to always consult the manufacturer's guide and ask for professional help if you are unsure. Developing and following a proper maintenance routine can keep your telescope in peak operating condition, ready to transport you to faraway cosmic locales at a moment's notice.

Remember, every star in the night sky is potentially within your reach with an immaculately maintained telescope. May your exploration of the universe continue unimpeded!

Chapter 11. Maximizing Your Stargazing Experience: Locations, Apps, and Other Resources

Finding the right location, leveraging technology, and utilizing the best resources is essential to maximize your stargazing experience. Even with an advanced telescope in hand, the lack of peripheral elements can significantly reduce the culmination of your celestial exploration. In this chapter, we'll discuss optimal locations for stargazing, introduce you to some must-have apps for astronomical adventures, and recommended resources to deepen your astronomy knowledge.

11.1. Optimal Locations for Stargazing

Choosing the right location for stargazing plays a pivotal role in enhancing the quality and scope of your observations. Here are some factors to consider:

1. Absence of Light Pollution: Prime stargazing spots usually boast a minimal city light encroachment. Urban lights can flood the sky with glaring brightness, severely obscuring your view of the stars. Seek areas away from populated cityscapes and brightly lit commercial zones for a clear and unobstructed stargazing experience.

2. High Altitude: Locations at a higher altitude typically offer better stargazing possibilities. Up there, the atmosphere is thinner, resulting in lesser atmospheric distortion and a far clearer view of the celestial bodies above.

3. Low Humidity: Areas with lower humidity levels will have fewer condensation and water particles in the atmosphere, facilitating a clearer view of the sky.

While suburban backyards can suffice for hobbyists, serious stargazers may want to take a trek to places with optimal stargazing conditions. Notable favorites include:

1. Mauna Kea, Hawaii: The highest point in Hawaii, yielding an unobstructed, panoramic view of the sky aided by a cloud inversion layer that keeps the sky clear.

2. Atacama Desert, Chile: one of the driest places on earth and home to several international astronomical observatories.

3. Aoraki Mackenzie, New Zealand: A recognized International Dark Sky Reserve, ideal for Southern Hemisphere viewing.

11.2. Stellar Apps for Stargazing

Marrying your stargazing adventure with the digitalworld can simplify your navigation across the star-filled canvas above. Here are some indispensable apps:

1. Stellarium: A planetarium for your device. It accurately shows the positions of stars, planets, and constellations, and can simulate both the night and day sky.

2. SkySafari: This app helps you locate stars, constellations, planets, and satellites. An added virtual reality mode lets you scan the sky with your device and identify the heavenly bodies through the camera feed.

3. Star Walk 2: This interactive astronomy guide permits you to observe in real-time what you would see in the sky above on a certain date at a certain time and place.

4. Google Sky: A browser-based application that lets you explore the farthest reaches of the starry sky and the universe from your web

browser.

11.3. Unveiling Astronomy: Essential Resources

Good resources can foster understanding and breed enthusiasm. Here are few must-have books and resources for every avid stargazer:

1. 'NightWatch: A Practical Guide to Viewing the Universe' – Renowned skygazer Terence Dickinson guides you through the nuances of stargazing in this easy read.

2. 'Turn Left at Orion' – A superb guide for amateur astronomers as it directly guides the user in observing and identifying stars and constellations.

3. Sky & Telescope Magazine: This monthly magazine delivers a wealth of information on astronomy with engaging content, great visuals, and how-to guides.

4. NASA's Website is a treasure trove of information and rich media content, a must for astronomy enthusiasts.

Whether you're using a high-tech telescope or binoculars, the pleasure of stargazing is always about being at the right place, at the right time, and with the right resources. By following the advice above, the universe is literally within your reach. So, don your astronomer's hat, look up, and conquer the cosmos.

www.ingramcontent.com/pod-product-compliance
Lightning Source LLC
Chambersburg PA
CBHW060855260726
48661CB00008B/3282